KATHI SMITH

REAL Budgeting Hacks

Learn how to quickly plan your paychecks, save money, pay off debt and achieve your financial goals - without the long-book fluff

Contents

Introduction

Welcome and congrats on your decision to take the brave step to build your financial future! Whether you're in your teens, twenties or forties, the decision to get serious about your hard earned dollars will give you an amazing sense of confidence, control and satisfaction.

My name is Kathi and I'm writing this book because I've experienced almost every emotion possible in regards to money. I was able to get a handle on my money and purchase my first home/rental property. I have a burning desire to help others by sharing what I've learned and implemented.

I want you to know that you *can* achieve your financial goals. I was not handed a silver spoon, nor did I inherit a million dollars to dabble with. I did, thankfully, inherit my mother's innate ability to budget. Did I always follow a budget? Heck no! Did I care? Heck no! I was just living life until I decided there had to be more to life than working, paying bills, getting a high paying job, working that job and paying higher bills. I woke up. I read a book called Rich Dad Poor Dad by Robert Kiysaki many years ago and was introduced to a new world of investing and passive income. Whoa! I could have money coming in without working my butt off for it every month? Sign me up! I wanted to invest, I wanted to own property, I wanted passive income, I wanted my own place...my own home - somewhere I could be free and make the rules.

Up until this point, I had made some pretty careless and naive choices with my money and credit because I didn't know how important they were. I was in a financial hole. I went from living in my own apartment, to moving in with friends, back to my own apartment (smaller and in a not so great part of town), finally to purchasing my first home and investment property. The process of getting your money and credit together takes work and patience and I want to save you from making pitfalls along the way. I want to share with you the exact steps I took to go from credit crappy to new home happy.

There were some things that I learned from investing seminars that were down right unbelievable to me at the time - like how to talk to creditors. Creditors used to scare me (honestly), but I learned how to take my power back when on creditor phone calls. It was a wild ride because they actually did what I said - we'll get to that later.

Disclaimer: I am not a financial advisor. I do advise you to seek help from financial advisors - just as I did. I am a person, just like you, that had *enough* of my time and efforts being given away to others in the form of dollars and online bill payments. I had budgeting skills, but sought advice from CPAs, credit counselors and multiple mortgage lenders.

This book is a condensed blueprint of how to gain more control of your life by gaining control of your finances. Doing this and maintaining your momentum will take instruction, but also a mindset change. This book is that instruction. The end of this book lists books that can help foster deep internal change. You need both. Don't get me wrong, you can follow these steps and get *great* results but end up back in the same rut if your mind and habits haven't truly changed - I know because it happened to me! I want the best for you, I want you to avoid this, so check out the books listed and find a few to read and apply.

Obviously, since you're here, you're ready…so let's do this!

WHO THIS BOOK IS AND ISN'T FOR

This book is for the person who doesn't want to read ten chapters before getting to the nitty- gritty of budgeting.

This book is for the person who likes bullet points instead of long paragraphs.

This book is for the person who likes to have things spelled out in a simple and easy to follow manner.

This book is for the person who wants truth - no matter how tough. (Yikes! It could get ugly.)

This book is NOT for the person who wants to sacrifice their goals for the fleeting joys of momentary pleasure.

This book is NOT for the person who is okay with spending away their most valuable assets - time and precious life.

This book is NOT for the person who is not willing to document their choices and progress to see the big financial picture.

So, now that you've read all that…is this book for you? I sure hope so!

Part 1 - The Buildup before the Breakdown

I grew up in a middle class family where my mother worked a 40-hour per week job at a local manufacturing plant, Champion Spark Plug, in Toledo, Ohio. She also had a Tupperware side hustle that I had no clue about growing up. Actually, my favorite toy dog, Bark Bark, was a company gift as one of the rewards for her awesome Tupperware sales. My dad also worked at the same manufacturing plant. My dad eventually started his own trucking company, where he worked even harder and often worked long hours.

My parents were hard workers and they were consistent. This combination provided us with food on the table and helped "put me through school" as my mom would say. They were also able to afford my teenage years' travels to China, Ghana, the Netherlands, Spain, Mexico, as well as yearly family trips "down south" for the summers. Why am I telling you this? Gloating, no. To paint the picture of a childhood with no financial worries and no financial discipline needed. I worked around the house every day and did extra chores on weekends, including washing dishes, dusting, vacuuming, cleaning my room, cleaning the bathroom, etc. I got an allowance, but I also got extra money from my dad when my allowance ran out. This helped reinforce a mindset that money would always come from *somewhere* if I needed it and there would be no consequence. My dad's love didn't require repayment with monthly interest.

My mother told me about not getting a credit card, but I didn't understand why, so naturally I got a credit card as soon as I went off to college. Yay! Instant money! Crazy far from the truth. Instant debt was more like it.

As the years passed, a few things happened. I

- met friends that were worse handling money than I was
- signed my name for cell phones these friends wanted (because my credit was still good)
- used my credit card to "help" others
- used my $300 credit card (Capital One) and accepted another credit card (Discover Card) with "no credit limit" I was told
- bought a pricey computer
- opened a few retail/department store credit cards
- skipped out on an apartment lease without paying the full lease term
- co-signed for a storage unit for one of my friends

I was happily ignoring most of my credit accumulations, living life, working a 40-hour per week job and splitting payments on a townhome that I shared with a roommate who I think got the place on a land contract (super freaking scam). Then the tide turned.

The threatening creditor letters started rolling in, nonstop. I was served a judgment that I would soon be garnished for the balance of the pricey computer I had purchased. I hadn't even heard of garnishment until this ordeal. I honestly didn't believe it would happen so I ignored the letter, like all the other snowballing debt problems. THEN IT HAPPENED!! I actually began getting garnished (a legal procedure in which a person's earnings are required by court order to be withheld by an employer for the payment of a debt) every paycheck. How could they do this to me? How could they just start *taking* money from *my* paycheck?? That's *my* money!

Over the next few years I learned the hard way that I was promising my time and money to others whenever I took on a new credit card, promise to pay or *any* debt account. I eventually moved out of that townhome due to unfortunate circumstances of increased roommates and the inability to feel safe and comfortable in my own place. I moved in with friends, a newly-married couple that had just bought a home on a nice side of town. I had a bedroom upstairs and used the full guest bathroom. I paid rent every month, being responsible in that area at least.

The threatening credit letters soon followed…how the heck did they find me??

I read Rich Dad Poor Dad, a book by Robert Kiyosaki and my eyes started to open…it was glorious and horrific at the same time. It was glorious to know that I could do more than just go to school, get a high paying job and have a bomb house with the proverbial picket fence. I could own property. I could have passive income. I had never really heard of passive income! Could I *really* do this? This sounded better than the Industrial age dogma I had grown up with. I loved my parents and will always respect their grind, but I didn't just want to have a good job for the rest of my life.

Side note: As I got older, I found out my parents owned single family rental properties. THEY NEVER, EVER MENTIONED THIS TO ME or as a possibility for my life.

After reading Rich Dad Poor Dad, I started reading other books about money and property investing. I didn't really understand that much about investing, but the mindset portion began to cause me to think differently and more consciously about money. I realized that I was in a messed up situation. I now had

- a car payment
- rent payment
- student loans
- rental debt collections at FABCO (rental debt collections agency)
- multiple open and charged off credit accounts
- a habit of buying whatever I wanted and using credit like eating candy.

After reading Rich Dad Poor Dad, I started to look for Robert Kiyosaki seminars since he was my new buddy now. There was a free real estate seminar, the Learn to Be Rich, Rich Dad Education training, hosted by his company coming to town so I reserved a spot and attended. They gave great scenarios of the wonders of real estate and what could be acquired. I was sold. They said they'd be back in town to host a more indepth seminar...for $435 dollars. Dang! Well okay, I could pay for that. So I did and I went and it was great, but then there was another seminar offered for over $1200 dollars and the prices kept getting higher and higher for more and more information and coaching. I got off the bus after the $435 seminar, but I learned such valuable information and received such valuable materials that I truly believe it was worth every dollar and more. During this seminar, they trained us on debt, creditors, getting our financial lives together and certain investment strategies.

As aforementioned, I was afraid of creditors and I let them harass me because I knew I owed them money and the garnishment took a lot of wind from beneath my wing. I didn't want any of these current creditors to do that to me again. I didn't know my rights and didn't know who to turn to, so this seminar gave me a huge confidence boost. I was armed with information and I was ready to change my life, a little at a time. I wanted to have my own place again. I wanted to be out of debt. I wanted to live a different life. I wanted to be free. And I actually started to believe it was possible.

If I wanted to live a different life, it was time to clean up my act.

Part 2 - The Collections Quick and Dirty: Credit, Creditors and Your Power

If you are reading this chapter, you may have experienced at least one of the debt situations described by the bullet points in the previous chapter. And if you have ever had accounts sent to collections, this is the chapter for you!

See No Evil

Ignoring and avoiding bills leads to a dead end in the credit world and negatively affects future hopes and dreams when it comes to relying on a good credit score for an important purchase. My credit score was down to 515 when I finally decided to take drastic actions. The following is what the seminars taught me about creditors and how to gain control of conversations when speaking to them. These points opened my eyes:

- When the original company *sells* your account to a collections company, the collections company pays pennies on the dollar for your account. *Pennies on the dollar.* This means the balance of $850 you owed the original company is not the balance you owe the collections company. In fact, it's a whole lot less! That's why they send letters saying "Pay your account in full today for $500. Act now because this offer expires yada yada." The $500 payoff amount is closer to the actual amount they bought your account for, and the percentages on the dollar go even lower than that. So when they call you threatening for the full amount, know that you can negotiate. "How?" you say, glad you asked.

- Keep *every* payoff offer letter from your creditors. I can't stress this enough. They will get more and more desperate, which means the payoff amount will become less and less. Great for you! But take caution to not wait too long if you have the means to pay the payoff amount. Pay it and move on to saving to pay your next account. I say this because I had a number of accounts and letters lined up and I couldn't pay them all at once, so I slowly paid one at a time while accumulating lower and lower offer letters from the other collections account holders.

- The creditor will honor the letter amount even past the offer expiration date. They want *something* in the form of money. If given the option of getting an account off their books they'll more than likely choose to receive the amount you offer them, which is the amount they actually offered you - no matter how long ago. Play your cards right, put on your best acting voice and confidently stand up for yourself when you make the phone call.

Here's a script you can use:

"Hi, I received a payoff letter for my account and I'm calling to pay off my balance."

They will ask for your information. They may say the offer expired.

You counter:

"I cannot pay the full balance and have another account that I need to pay. I chose to call _(current company name)_ first because I can afford to pay the full payoff balance. If you will not accept my payment, I will call the other account and leave this one in collections."

If they still object, you can say:

"Thank you for your help. I'd like to speak to a manager/supervisor that has the authority to make this decision."

Then wait. There is always someone higher up that can make the decision to accept your payoff amount. When the manager/supervisor gets on the phone, use the exact same script with them. One of two things will happen. They will gladly accept your payment or you will not pay them at all.

TIP: Stand your ground!
   Don't accept an offer to make payment arrangements for the full amount.
   Never feel bad about not getting the issue resolved with the first call.

For the most part, you will be able to pay less and get the account out of your hair. IF they don't accept your offer, move on to the next account holder.

I've had friends go as far as acting as if their spouse was crazy/abusive and didn't want them to pay their debts and they were "sneaking" to make the call to pay the collections company. The crazy spouse was yelling in the background. It worked! Desperate times call for desperate measures!

This strategy worked like a dream for me, although for one company, I had to set up payment arrangements, BUT the payment arrangement was for the payoff amount and *not* for the full amount. Still a win!

- ALWAYS keep proof of every account you satisfy/pay off because you will need it to send a copy to the three credit bureaus - TransUnion, Equifax and Experian. Ask for a letter, emailed or mailed. Ask for a confirmation number. Write the date, time, representative's name and confirmation number right on the payoff letter in your hand and keep it for your records until you get the actual proof from the company.

- When you receive your payoff letters from the companies, make copies and send them to the three major credit bureaus. Ask them to update/remove these derogatory accounts from your credit statement. There are plenty of websites and Youtube videos that can instruct you how to word these requests. Pick one and get at it!

You are on your way…how do you feel?

When you get to this point, congratulate yourself - you deserve it. You are responsibly working toward your greater financial future!

Put these steps on repeat until your credit report looks light and airy. Creditors report monthly, so results may not be noticeable immediately, but after a handful of good months, you'll start to look better and better on paper.

Be encouraged! Keep your goals in mind. You got this!

These things affect your credit score positively:

- On-time payments. Suck it up and do it.
- Certain big ticket accounts - your rent, mortgage, car note and utility on-time payments.

Did you know? If you are unable to pay your utility bill, the company may have a relief program that lets you pay a portion of your amount spread over time. Did I mention I sold electricity services after the electric utility monopoly became deregulated? Yep, I was in a network marketing group for that, trying to make quick money. It's safe to say I've almost tried it all - except the seedy things, which I seriously considered at one point - just saying.

You will see your score rise slowly and steadily or more quickly depending on what type of action you take. My credit education and cleanup took about three to five good years. Yours can take more or less time depending on your situation and how much you are able to push yourself.

How the heck am I going to make these credit payments? You ask.

In the current economic atmosphere of quick startups, new entrepreneurs and people that want to "fire their boss", I have real and sobering news. Don't quit your day job. I can say this because I tried it myself (told you I've tried almost everything) and it ain't what it's cracked up to be. Just think about it. How are you going to keep a roof over your head, food in the fridge, transportation (even if it's a bus pass-which I have bought many) and work on your financial future? You MUST ask yourself, can I quit my job right now and be fully able to take care of myself? Do I have enough money saved to pay my bills if the cash flow from my business isn't flowing like milk and honey? Be honest. Don't put yourself in a worse situation. Work that job, make that overtime money, do the side hustle hustle (that's my term for turn up the productivity in your side hustle) and *lightly* treat yourself in the midst of it all. You've got goals to achieve. Sacrifice today to have better tomorrows. The years are coming, just like this year came. Where will you be when they come? Hopefully, after reading this book and taking action, in a *much* better place!

Part 3 - Paycheck Budgeting: The Nitty-Gritty

I t's finally time to get down to budgeting and planning nitty-gritty. This, my friends, is where you will learn to shine, or at least glisten a little more than usual.

This section is divided into steps to make it easier to mentally consume and apply. Also, you are welcome to use the links provided for materials that will help you budget and plan if additional resources are needed.

The point of a budget is twofold - to manage your money coming in (income) and the money going out of your pocket/account. You want to become uber aware of what you are doing with your income.

Fish Nets

Are your pockets fish nets? No, not the sexy women's pantyhose from the 80s. I mean, are your funds coming in and immediately draining out? Do you know where all of your funds are going every week? Is there too much month at the end of the money? Do you find yourself borrowing money from others *often*? Do you find yourself at check cashing stores?

Side note: I actually did the check cashing thing to help friends out… repeatedly. Check cashing is a vicious cycle. Don't get caught in it. Enough said.

It's time for a budget.

Tips and Hacks

Quick TIPS and HACKS for budgeting:

- Use cash (critical hack). This helps you see and *feel* the money coming in and leaving your person.
- Use the envelope system (optional). Look this up on Youtube to find tons of instructional videos.
- Say "no" more to extra curricular activities
- Eat before you eat. If you decide to occasionally go out to eat with friends or family, eat at home first. I've done this many times and saved a *ton* by just ordering soup or salad and eating the free bread placed on the table. I've even just drank water and told everyone I couldn't stay long enough for the entrees and just wanted to enjoy the conversation before leaving. Do whatcha gotta do to do whatcha gotta do.
- Buy less expensive alternatives. For example, I bought a pan, just your average pan to cook food, from Family Dollar that lasted three years. I've bought nice dishes from the Dollar Tree…how will they know? You'd be surprised at Dollar Tree finds *and* you'll save money. Keep in mind, this stage is only temporary. Your come-up is coming.
- Talk to a financial professional during your financial repair and

success journey. Laws change, reporting may change, loopholes may be found. You don't know what you don't know, so get in the know. What you learn can change the course of your journey.

- Revisit your budget regularly - weekly, bi-weekly and however often you need. You should realistically be looking at your budget at least once a week and making any adjustments to saving, spending, etc.

- Open an untouchable direct deposit savings account at a different bank with no card access (or give the card to someone else) so you must drive to the bank to get the money. When you think about what it takes to get the money out of the account for a purchase, it should make you stop and think "Okay, is getting this _______ that serious?"

Siphon as little or as much into this account from every paycheck automatically, without having to see it. Let it build in the background.

- Use the credit card payoff system explained later in this section.
- Bonus Kick in the butt to help you: write down *every* dollar amount you spend outside of bills for two months then assess your spending habits - yikes! I realized I was spending close to $350 a month on going out to eat, "helping" pay for other's meals and on random snacks at work. The heck?! Was I really doing that?! The numbers don't lie so I had to come to grips with the truth, quickly. That spending had to stop. I forced myself to start buying more groceries. I also bought quick snacks that I could grab, go and store in my car if I got the munchies while out or at work. I like helping people, so I felt wrong for stopping this, but my new mindset told me that the more I was responsible with money now, the more I could *truly* help others in the future. Keep in mind that when you continue to "help" others that make their own poor financial decisions, you are

being a crutch to them and stopping them from feeling the pain of their choices. Sometimes the best thing you can do for individuals is say "no", believe me they will find another way.

Let's get down to your budget:

Step 1 - Use a visual system that is simple and easy to access.

This could be pen and paper, an Excel Spreadsheet, a Google sheet, a Google doc, or whatever works best for you. Remember, your job is not to learn a new skill and figure out how to use new budgeting software. When you get into investing and using a financial statement, the advanced recording systems will be very helpful. Right now, your job is to find a simple way to accurately track your money. It's as simple as that.

Step 2 - List *every single thing* you pay for, including monthly subscriptions and all.

I was recently working with a couple on getting their monthly budget together and they were blown away when they saw *all* the things they were paying for on a list right in front of them. There is power in bringing awareness to what is going on in our lives. In addition, list the due dates of every expense/bill.

Step 2 will take some work because you need to do research. Please don't pay for an app that can track your spending across different apps.

This is just another expense. You have the ability to dedicate the time and effort it takes to do this on your own. I believe in you. It's actually a very rewarding process, in an eye-opening sort of way.

Step 3 - Decide what you *need* to live vs. what you *want* to live.

Needs are items such as rent/mortgage, car payments, insurance, utilities, groceries and phone. Wants are mostly everything else. Active credit card bills stay on this list unless you simply cannot pay them at all.

Next, Circle or highlight your wants and take a deep dive into your reasons for having them. Realize that they are stealing from your future financially happier self, then make some tough decisions on what can be cut. Place an "X" on what you plan on cutting and cut them immediately.

Warning: This may be a bit painful, because these expenses are usually tied to our emotions, but after the cut *and* after seeing the positive effect it has on your monthly budget, you will be thankful.

Step 4 - Take a moment to see how your monthly budget looks with and without your wants.

You feeling a bit better? Yes, you are on your way now! Decide to cut the extra for good or for a specific period of time. Go hard and give yourself a full year away from your extras then reassess your need for them. You may be surprised at what can wait while you are on the way to your financially fit future.

Step 5 - Fill in your new monthly budget, week by week.

Seeing your finances in a monthly layout gives you a visual, while seeing your finances in a weekly layout gives you instruction. You will know exactly what needs to be paid and when. You can also automate this process by using the autopay option offered by many companies. Use whatever method of payment works for you. Personally, I use a mixture of autopay and self pay because I get a monthly discount when using the autopay option on certain bills. Check to find out if you can take advantage of this simple money-saving hack. Every dollar you keep counts.

Be sure to put your expenses in dated order. For example, if your rent is due on the 1st and your car payment is due on the 10th, your rent should be higher on the sheet/table than your car payment.

Ex:

Bill & due date__________Amount

Rent - 5th$1000
   Car payment - 10th$350
   Car insurance - 20th $150
   Cell phone/Internet -25th $240

Finally, fill in your after tax, take home income amount at the very top of your sheet/table. Do not include bonuses or any similar additional monies. You want to know exactly what you're working with, so this amount should be consistent and predictable.

Use bonuses, tax return funds and unexpected monies to pay down the primary debt account you will choose to focus on. It's also okay to spend a bit of this cash on yourself. You deserve it for being so diligent.

Step 6 - Do the math

This is a very sobering moment. You are now looking at your new, improved plan for the future.

Where else can you make adjustments? Modify your plan as needed.

Congrats, you are gaining ground!

Monthly Budget Sheet

July

Due

7/5

7/12

7/19

7/26

Paycheck

$2000

$2000

Additional income

Total

2000

2000

Tithe/
 Donation

200

200

Rent/
 mortgage
 900
 5th
 900

-

Car payment
 350
 10th
 350

-

Car Insurance
20th
150
-

150

Life insurance
250
20th
-

250

Car gas

200
100

100

Electric bill

100
20th
-

100

Gas bill

100

  20th

  -

100

Cell phone,

  Internet

  240

  25th

  -

240

Credit card

  #1

  70

  27th

  -

70

Credit card

  #2

  30

  27th

-

30

Groceries

300
100

200

Savings

200

400

Personal Needs & Entertainment

50

100

Total

1900

1940

What's Left

100 allocate
  where needed

60 allocate where needed

Step 7 - **Add your goal items**

Do you want to take a trip, do something on your bucket list, or add a few extra items to your wardrobe? Add this to your budget. Use this model - say you want to save $1000 for a trip, ask yourself:

- Is this a trip that can wait until next year?
- How will taking this trip help me?
- How will not taking this trip negatively affect me? Be honest.

If you still decide to take the trip or do the thing, next ask yourself:

- Can this $1000 be downsized at all?
- If so, how?

Add this to your monthly budget incrementally. For example, you're able to downsize to $750, you can save $125 toward your trip every month over the course of six months.

Step 8 - Take action! Take control!

You've made it this far, now it's time to follow through. You can do it! Cut the extra expenses! Make the extra money! Follow through for a better financial you!

This information is not new, nor is it groundbreaking, but use it consistently and you will position yourself to begin investing in profitable ventures. There are various ventures available that will put passive income into your pockets, but that is a topic for another book. *This* is your stepping stone. Start here and work your way towards your goals and future dreams.

I have composed a list of mindset books and investment strategy books that will help you develop your inner habits, your financial IQ and your outlook on investing. In addition, I'd like to share a few points that I've learned from wealthy individuals along the way.

Common thinking vs. Wealthy thinking

Get a good educationGet a good financial education

Seek job security and work for moneyMoney works for me

Plan only paychecksPlan wealth for generations

Worry if not getting a raise Build wealth with excitement

Buy a big houseBuy income producing property

Save moneyInvest money

The credit card payoff system

If you have credit card debt and you feel like paying the minimum monthly payments are killing you, I get it. I felt the same way. I felt like I was getting nowhere with my credit card payments until I learned this system years ago.

Pay your credit cards off faster with this simple system:

Look at the interest rates on your credit cards and find the one with the highest interest rate. Interest is the money you are literally giving away on top of paying back what was borrowed. It's the price paid to the credit company for giving you right-now funds. (You can actually call your credit card company to get your interest rate decreased, which is another great hack.) It's enough to make you mad when you realize how much of your monthly payment actually goes to pay the principal balance vs. the interest.

Work on paying this account off first by paying more than the minimum payments every month. Whether it's $20 or $200, this will knock down the *principal* amount every month which is super helpful. Continue to pay the minimum on your other cards.

When this card is paid off, congratulate yourself and move to the next account. On your budget sheet/chart, keep this monthly amount as a bill, but add it to your next highest interest bearing account. It will look like this:

Month 1

Bill & due date___________Amount

Cr card A - 5th$350 - 1st to pay off
   Cr card B - 10th$50 - 2nd to pay off
   Cr card C - 12th $50 - last to pay off/down

Month 5

Bill & due date___________Amount

Cr card A - 5th$0 - 1st to pay off
   Cr card B - 10th$400 - 2nd to pay off ($50+$350= $400)
   Cr card C - 12th $50 - last to pay off/down

Month 8

Bill & due date___________Amount

Cr card A - 5th$0 - 1st to pay off
   Cr card B - 10th$0 - 2nd to pay off
   Cr card C - 12th $450 - last to pay off/down ($50 +$50+$350= $450)

Keep the card with the lowest interest open, to help build your credit score. Use it for gas or something you have the cash to afford, then make payments on that card. Lenders are looking to see how well you keep your credit usage under 30% of the allowable credit limit.

Conclusion

No matter where you start, you can achieve your financial goals and create an amazing financial future. You have the power to take control of your money by putting in time, effort and by applying the strategies outlined in this book. Once you begin seeing your finances shift and your credit score increase, you'll feel a wonderful sense of relief and confidence in your ability to achieve your financial goals. Always consider your well-being in the midst of your journey. Remember self-care and take time to reward yourself along the way.

I'm excited for your success and for the growth you are bound to experience while taking control of your money helps you take more control of your *greatest* asset - your time. It's time to go for it, you financial goal getter!

If you found this book helpful, I'd be appreciative if you left a favorable review for the book on Amazon!

Kindest regards,

Kathi

Book Recommendation List

Rich Dad Poor Dad by Robert Kiyosaki

Cash Flow Quadrant by Robert Kiyosaki

The Millionaire Next Door by Thomas J. Stanley and William D. Danko

Eat That Frog! by Brian Tracy

Time Management by Brian Tracy

See You at the Top by Zig Ziglar

Get Good with Money by Tiffany Aliche the Budgetnista

Secrets of Six-Figure Women by Barbara Stanny

The Total Money Makeover by Dave Ramsey

The Psychology of Winning by Dennis Waitley

Developing Winner's Habits by Dennis Waitley

Seeds of Greatness by Dennis Waitley

Why We Want You to Be Rich by Donald J. Trump and Robert Kiyosaki

The Secret Language of Money by David Krueger, M.D. with John David Mann

The 12 Week Year by Brian P. Moran and Michael Lennington

Resources

Garnishment. (n.d.). DOL. https://www.dol.gov/general/topic/wages/garnishments

Kiyosaki, R. T. (2009). *Rich dad, poor dad: What the rich teach their kids about Money—That the poor and the middle class do not!* http://ci.nii.ac.jp/ncid/BA50082780

Ramsey, D. (2009). *The total money makeover: A Proven Plan for Financial Fitness.* Thomas Nelson Inc.

Robintek. (2022, July 1). *Homepage - FABCO Tenant Screenings & Rental Collections.* FABCO Tenant Screenings & Rental Collections. https://fabcogroup.com/